Praise for Shirley Geok-lin Lim

"Anyone expecting age and a lifetime of educational and poetic achievement to have mellowed Shirley Lim will be rocked by *Dawns Tomorrow*. In this panorama of short lyrics, she is still Geok-lin Lim, the girl from Melaka, "baggage in my head stored / for life" (in both senses of "for life"); still wrestling with a complex, internationally-minded identity; still searching for "Poetry and Justice." Her tussle with "words not yet mastered" is very much a woman's way of "dressing down to my naked core," but she, like Gandhi, finds "radiance" and even humor in simplicity and memories. This is not, though, a poetry of nostalgia; her intense curiosity and intelligence have her and the reader looking to "Dawns" and "Tomorrow." All her work is "a threat to sameness."

—Dennis Haskell
Author of nine collections of poetry, most recently *And Yet…* (WA Poets Publishing, 2020), plus fourteen volumes of literary scholarship and essays

"What an abundance of new poems from Shirley Lim: a feast like those recalled from her Malaysian childhood—*gula melaka, rojak, nasi lemak*—or like the bounty of her adult life in southern California, where ripe oranges and lemons litter the very sidewalks. But the speaker of these poems is caught between those two worlds: an abusive childhood and an alienating adulthood where she must grapple with racism, and watch the political situation grow increasingly threatening. Salvation comes from the act of writing ("Hello, white page! Hello, dear possible!") and from the bonds of motherhood ("The hurt child will always be hurt. But she will grow up to become the good mother.") Sharp-eyed and mercilessly honest in her dissection of self and society—yet at times, very funny!—Lim is at the peak of her powers in this generous, rewarding collection."

—Julie Kane
Louisiana Poet Laureate, winner of Academy of American Poets Prize, National Poetry Series, and Donald Justice Prize. Her most recent poetry collection is *Mothers of Ireland*

"Reading *Dawns Tomorrow*, we marvel at Shirley Geok-lin Lim's unfailing ability to capture moments small and momentous in the sharpest and most direct way. The unflinching bravery in her writing shines through the collection. From the potent brevity of "School Shooting" to the contemplative generosity in the "Re-visiting" poems, we have a poet whose language is chiseled and style varied. The Hong Kong poems, though few, are powerful, especially "Admiralty," which reads like a definitive work about the city's recent pro-democracy protests ("Five years have passed, / each year in Hong Kong, someone's last."). I have read Lim's poetry for over two decades, and *Dawns Tomorrow* surprises me with its raw newness. Long may this newness live."

— Tammy Lai-Ming Ho
Founding co-editor of *Cha: An Asian Literary Journal*, editor of *Hong Kong Studies*, the first peer-reviewed journal devoted to Hong Kong

"In lifelong exile, Shirley Geok-lin Lim writes new poems from countries and islands all over the world. Her awed voice reaches our ears, and we get to know ourselves from myriad views."

— Maxine Hong Kingston
Poet, memoirist, and fiction writer whose honors include the National Medal of Arts and the National Humanities Medal

"Shirley Lim searches for hope and home as she moves around the globe.... she evokes and makes palpable a peace in the natural world's demands, resilience and beauty."

— Florence Howe
Founding Director and Publisher of the Feminist Press, author of *A Life in Motion*, editor of *No more masks!* and other collections

"(Lim's) poetry [is] a rare achievement...Like Wallace Stevens, she has put a planet on the table, a homemade world of her own experience... a poet of exile and assimilation, loss and recovery, journeys and explorations."

— Dana Gioia
California Poet Laureate and Chairman of the National Endowment for the Arts

Dawns Tomorrow

Poems by

Shirley Geok-lin Lim

Sungold Editions • Santa Barbara
2024

Published by Sungold Editions

Cover painting: "Autumn - On the Hudson River" (1860).
    Jasper Francis Cropsey (artist) American, 1823 - 1900.
    Courtesy National Gallery of Art, Washington

Author photo © 2021 Mia Nie

ISBN-13: 979-8-9867290-8-4

"The poem is the still point in a turning world"

By Lauri Scheyer

In an era when chapbooks or slim poetry volumes (often thematically or stylistically focused) are a frequent standard, Shirley Geok-lin Lim's new book is an audaciously monumental compilation. In her twelfth poetry collection (added to a library shelf's worth of novels, a memoir, short stories, critical studies, edited anthologies, and special journal issues), we encounter a writer's writer in the truest sense of those words. The word is Lim's purchase on the world, and we readers are blessed for her company, observations, intellect, insight, love, and wisdom as our literary companion and guide.

Contrary to the popular maxim, this book's cover sheds important light on what lies within. Before reading the description from the New York Metropolitan Museum of Art, which houses the painting "Autumn—On the Hudson River, 1860" by Jasper Francis Cropsey, I had written "monumental" to describe Lim's new manuscript. It is fortuitous but no coincidence to discover that the National Gallery used the same word to describe the painting that Lim has chosen to illuminate the poems. Commentary on this painting offers a valuable perspective on *Dawns Tomorrow* and the aptness of this cover art, including its geographical resonance in the poet's life:

> This monumental view of the Hudson River Valley was painted from memory in the artist's London studio. Cropsey adopted a high vantage point, looking southeast toward the distant Hudson River and the flank of Storm King Mountain.... signs of man's peaceful coexistence with nature:...both coexist harmoniously. In fact, the landscape is depicted as a ready arena for further agricultural expansion.... Cropsey's painting is more a celebration of American nationalism. As a critic wrote in 1860, the picture represents "not the solemn wasting away of the year, but its joyful crowning festival."

Cropsey's "Autumn—on the Hudson River" provides a fitting metaphor for *Dawns Tomorrow*. The carefully dated poems from past eras reveal that they were "recollected in tranquility" (Wordsworth) and serve as portraits of moments emblazoned in the poet's consciousness. The poems' vantage point is often from a distance, allowing minutely observed telling details. Signs of peaceful coexistence with nature are a signature of Lim's poetry, and this collection is replete with appreciation of Earth's bounty and beauty. A poet writing in the autumn of her life, the poems here depict this season, as in Cropsey's painting, as a "joyful crowning festival."

The opening poem, "Hello," is an invocation, an epistle, and an apostrophe to the white page. The terror of many poets, the white page is tenderly a "dear possible," a listed multiplicity of roles for the addressee: friend, sage, child, stranger "whose language comes from afar," a "fire just breaking/in dry brush that will burn the old world," the classical deity Diana the huntress poised to shoot, and ultimately, "self, untutored, reading your blank gaze," fusing page and poet in a single identity. A renowned scholar-critic-professor and a prescient commentator on Asian-American, postcolonial, women's studies, and ethnic studies, the self-reflexive appellation of "untutored" is characteristic of Lim's humility and attitude of perpetual openness to life's continuing lessons.

Of the collection's four sections—"Preludes," "Eggshells," "Walking Alone," and the title section containing the title poem, "Dawns Tomorrow" —"Preludes," the longest section, is in many ways a preliminary setting of the historical and cultural stage for the following, more overtly "present-day." Lim writes, "Of the four sections, the first 'Preludes' has a few poems coming out of an earlier Asian homeland— Malaysia, Singapore, Hong Kong—, but most of 'Preludes' covers my New York identities, that are sourced in the Hudson River currents and banks. The second 'Eggshells' arrives from the socio-political angst of these times, the third 'Walking Alone' finds the resilience in that image, and the final 'Dawns Tomorrow' speaks from an American perspective of uplift and wry transcendence, that candle of democracy 'blowing in the wind.'"

While it would be a mistake to read poems in "Preludes" as "Asian" or even explicitly "Asian American poems," this in no way implies a rejection or denial of her history or heritage. But even in the poem "Before and After Leaving." the speaker refers to "a language/long foreign even then/in the lands where it'd/come," which yet remains "this mnemonic/ whereby my lyric is strung." Lim's literary vision is the composite of her totality of experiences where a dominant tonal hallmark is always the strength and will to move forward, to keep dancing. Music, movement, and embrace of life suffuse this fundamentally uplifting collection.

The bold array of forms, styles, and themes results in a collection with consistently delightful surprises, its stunning range uniformly handled with originality and technical deftness. The separate sections are ingeniously movable components geographically and chronologically, but common links identify all these poems, regardless of their impressively varying styles and forms, as derived from the same poetic mind. Two words particularly apt in describing the poems are "plenitude" and "inquisitiveness."

We find myriad structures and tones that result in a book that feels like both a journal and a journey. For example, there are odes ("Praise of Moon Cakes") and a literary pastiche in a response poem to Donne's "A Valediction Forbidding Mourning" suggesting the poet's impressive dexterity in evoking geography and culture to serve her muse. Several overtly political poems show Lim's perspicuous take on government and power as well as her dry wit, such as "Don Giovanni in the U.S." starring an operatic Donald Trump. "The Long Arc," where "Plain spoken poetry/ has no home," is a powerful indictment in short staccato lines built on the ominous extended metaphor of a swinging rope. We find philosophical musings in poems that are unafraid to ask unanswerable questions such as "Why is It?" which effectively foregrounds the figure of anaphora. "Must History?" is another poignant poem foregrounding the poignant form of the question. The gorgeously imagistic poem "Ripeness" evokes William Carlos Williams. "Dear Madam" is a sly commentary on womanhood, one of several epistolary poems in the collection in addition to the opening poem mentioned. We even find beautiful contemporary villanelles in "Hoarder's Dreams" and "No Accounting."

We see her skill in examining and playing with the operations of language and linguistic shift in "Mongering," where Lim explores the evolution and permutations of that word. "Daylight Savings," one of several prose poems that breaks down the absurdities of contemporary culture, is an Ashbery-like romp in multiple voices about that missing hour and what is or isn't "saved." "This Unsceptered isle, Singapura" provides imagistic word association in short choppy lines explicitly connecting food with the act of writing. Kitchens, cooking, gardens, celebration—eating, serving, and sharing meals and food suffuse this collection. In the poem, "Plenty," the child within remains vividly alive in this cornucopia of details about buying leftover stale cupcakes. Including this poem in the book's opening section helps set the stage for the laden gardens and tables spilling with repeated rituals and celebrations that enrich the whole collection with a profusion of sensory and social descriptions.

In what she calls her "ordinary life," Lim summarizes her identity in a message to me, "I am an assimilated American, an identity with little purchase in today's USA 'mosaic' but my daily reality. My neighbors are 'white,' Hispanic, Taiwanese, South Asian, Armenian, Jews, first-generation immigrants from the UK, Scotland, the PRC, Madagascar, Jamaica, and of course from Kansas, Texas, Nebraska, etc. While I always walk alone, these neighbors enjoy chatting!" In this phantasmagoria, we experience what is representatively American. The allying feature is the poet's voice, perspective, and identity. It is a rare volume of poetry that generates such a strong sense of a poet taking us by the hand and walking us through her life. We trust her to open our minds and eyes to something new and illuminating. Rather than the debased standard of the familiar or the "relatable," Lim does something more important: she refreshes our vision with startling insights and perspectives, which is the real job of poetry.

This is an American collection, a New York collection, a California collection, a woman's collection, an educator's collection—yet these poems would not be what they are without the earlier life experiences and Lim's cross-cultural background which has continued to play out in the international present of her family, friends, and both the local and global circles in which she travels. Although they are explicitly lyric poems in the American canonical tradition, they also contain a narrative thread which is the continuing journey of the poet's life. Poems range from walking to school in Pengkalan Rama to metaphorically walking on eggshells to walking alone while chattering with friendly neighbors along the way. The poems travel from taking the train to New York's Grand Central Station and ending up on the West Coast, all the while preparing food, gazing at the moon, gaining a vocabulary for and in America, and wondering what we are entitled from life regardless of our location. The title poem offers us a seeming paradox that is also a key to this book's premise: "Dawns tomorrow surprise with repetition." While a lesser poet might see tedium and predictability in recurring phenomena, Lim shows us that the dawns of all our tomorrows have new surprises to reveal if we remain open to their teachings. For Lim, the poem is indeed "the still point in a turning world" where we are privileged to be invited to join her.

Lauri Scheyer is the author of *A History of African American Poetry* and *Slave songs and the Birth of African American Poetry*, editor of *Theatres of War* and *The Heritage Series of Black Poetry, 1962-1975*. Currently Xiaoxiang Scholars Distinguished Professor, Hunan Normal University, she is founding director of the British and American Poetry Research Center. She is also Professor Emeritus at Cal State LA, where she was the founding director of the Center for Contemporary Poetry and Poetics.

For Charles Bazerman, for the good years

Contents

WALKING ALONE

DAWNS TOMORROW

Hello

Hello, white page! Hello, dear possible!
I greet you as friend open to questions.
I greet you as sage, silent, never
to speak. I greet you as my child,
stammering, words not yet mastered,
tears in your eyes. Greet you as stranger
whose language comes from afar, lisping,
guttural, whose speakers have scattered.
I greet you as fire just breaking
in dry brush that will burn the old world.
Greet you, towering Diana, arrow
tipped to the target. I greet you as
Self, untutored, reading your blank gaze.

PRELUDES

Before and After Leaving

(Dedicated to Melaka)

Before and After: I never
knew it as a child. Not that
exact phrase. Learned it
in the days that followed.
Each day remarkable
moments: nothing if not
its self; all presence.
Streets reduced to
the incurious narrow
river meeting salt sea
in slow sedimentation.
Two hills, ruined walls,
tall standing tombstones,
overwritten in a language
long foreign even then
in the lands where it'd
come. Foreign in
ancient hometown ruin,
inland waters' low
gullies, the *before*
and after like single
days strung on present
absence—this mnemonic
whereby my lyric is strung.

Christmas Prayer

Half a century plus, you've
diminished from the man who bore
my three-year-old wriggly
body above the Straits' clear waves.
I've lived another fifty
plus years without you, your
remembered complexity—
tender paternity,
cruelty—almost vanished
trauma. Except this moment's
prayer for the spirit I've
troubled, vanquished
with unavailing love,
unavailing accusation,
to be able to compose,
as I hope will be written
of me, rest in peace.

Convent Lessons

      Old nun of a piano teacher
rapped my wayward fingers
with a fierce wooden ruler,
stopped the music one hot afternoon.
      Giddy young art teacher,
smiling, knuckled my head,
dammed my flowing colors to red-
eyed teary smeary trickles.
      Bible Studies teacher
stood me on a high stool,
chalk in mouth and drip-drool
on blouse. Pushed me out the room
to stand all day, children watching,
obedient.
      She turned my eyes
away from her ruled lies,
white on blackboard. *Listen!*
      The bad child who
pinched when I cried, taught me
by the class door: *Turn! See
your Muses, Poetry and Justice.*

Plenty

Day-old cupcakes, pink and yellow icing
crusted, still dainty on shelves, leftovers,
two for five cents, coin for my morning
bus ride to school three miles away, squeezed
past *Pengkalan Rama*'s tile-roofed Chinese
merchant houses, crossing the bridge over
the trickle that once was a mighty river,
skirting Morrises, lorries, and trishaws,
outgrown tennis shoes squelching through puddles,
the hike, like the sun rising, swift, heat like a saw
blistering sweat, while each day-old cupcake
dissolves a slow trickling plenty to slake
everything, two cupcakes against young feet
crushed in canvas, walking the hungry street.

This unsceptered isle, *Singapura*

Vegetable: *chili padi.*
Animal: poisonous prawn.
Mineral: rough stone
cut, polished ruby.

Heartland fast-food paradise:
multivocal hawkers—*rojak,*
dosai, nasi lemak, Hainan
chicken rice.

Associative chain
work-in-progress:
epic content,
short form, riven.

Regulated measure:
contradiction-tension
written in present tense, to
future-tense pleasure.

National University of Singapore Morning Run

Brave mossies and sun.
Circle the field.

Busses whirl by perimeters,
run of cars, unseen commuters
set for long labor hours.

White gulls drop by to feed on grubs
in greensward, another pastoral
subs for distant managers.

Make bucolic what lurks
regulated regular. Verdant
field mimics the mind-field

synergy, just like equator sweat-
smells soak this city-slick campus.

A USP Valediction Forbidding Mourning

With thanks to John Donne's "A Valediction Forbidding Mourning"
(For USP Poets, 2012)

AS weary teachers end their modules and leave,
    To *ivle** their students goodbye,
While some of these poets post brief
    Lyrics on Facebook, and some sigh,

So let us read poetry with no tweaks,
    No word-deletes, nor line breaks move;
It would prove the poem slack and weak
    To tell the readers we disapprove.

Moving of the stanzas brings angst and tears;
    Poets over-analyze what it did, and meant;
But flying off this hemisphere,
    Though greater far, is innocent.

Non-deep-breathing poets' posts
    —Whose aim is sense—can only admit
Of semester's end as loss
    Of the thing which drew them first.

But we by a poetics so much refined,
    That ourselves know how rich it is
Residing in our collective mind,
    Will not class and workshop miss.

Your poems therefore, which are one
    Collection, though I must go, endure not

Bad reviews, but enjoy extension,
    With every fresh poem's joyful beat.

If teachers and students be two, they are
    Two so as brave trekkers are two;
The elder, seeming fixed, must dare
    To move, in order that the other grow.

And though teacher on United flies off,
    Yet when the student emails come,
She'll lean to read and count the soft
    Syllables of their Singapore home.

So are you USP poets to me, who must,
    Like Emily's poems, obliquely run;
Your words have made my visit just,
    To make me end where I'd begun.

* *ivle* The USP internet program in 2012 for coursework

On the Ferry to Macau

Across the bow's indistinct dark
horizon, increasing lumpy clay
thickens brown beach, green bark,
stone, pebble.
        Gray in the bay
is salt, land-sighted, sandy
encoded ancestral DNA.

Neither fisher nor refugee,
we are borne on turbojets' spray
buffeting wake of cruisers, lighters,
tugs.
        Dreams of islands jostle, sway
on all sides barely above water,
bearing stray Nanyang farers.

Praise of Moon Cakes

The round brown cakes litter
supermarket counters, melon-
crunchy-seeded, lard-svelte,
slick sesame or red bean paste.
At their center orange yolks burst
in salty shards. Mid-Autumn
promises all this—children
seeding Hong Kong streets, glitter
of fat wallets amidst
the sweet spread of women.
Its core a golden yolk,
moon cake to be sliced
and shared. We lift our wine, iced
for September, like Tang poets
barred from the Forbidden
City, companioning the harvest
moon, as she shines on reaping and barren
salt flats, generous to all creation.

Admiralty

(2014, 2019)

Five years have passed, five long years, and still
planes land and lift off the tarmac, hills
not yet dwarfed by thickening towers
filling up and emptying of people,
fixed unstable on sea and land however
mixed.
        Five years and still the children's chants
echo in the millions' multi-level haunts.
Its canyons' windows open to grannies
watchful of children's children, the city's
uncles, grandpas in wheelchairs, aunts
who had been schoolgirls five years ago.

        Two million on the march is slow
motion exercise of a people's will.
Avenues in black, black and white: what ills
occupy the world's channels? Their mono-
chrome grief is grievance against tomorrow's
losses.
        The bosses' gambles are sorrow
sowed in a wind not of their election.
The young sing in English elocution,
rally in Cantonese, day-dream horror
sci-fi future worlds.
        Five years have passed,
each year in Hong Kong someone's last.

To an Asian American Academic

From Hong Kong, your eyes swim and peer
behind glasses half an inch thick. Black
turtleneck & skirt. Short straight hair
halves your little face. Do you remember
wearing black is asking for death?

I dreamt we were picking
shellfish—clams, mollusks, oysters. They fall
off our baskets, and we backtrack
to find them, two women who've given
ourselves to language, serious & useful,
like gentlemen, when no one knows what sack
of shells to put us in.
                              We bend, pick, drop.
The dream is hard work, fresh shucked, un-end-stopped.

Drench

Plops and flashes, shaking fronds.
I'd forgotten natural
violence. Roof holds. Ceilings keep
ancient stains.
                    What if walls
shriek apart, cyber ghosts transfer,
house shifts to catastrophe?

What if vaults collapse, papers,
certs, banknotes, contracts fly in
tornadoes of time failed,
back to children meeting
despair and going on:
                    can
a scoop of porridge cup pleasure
so minor it fills their tiny
bellies and spills into the world
outside the vanished home?

Will the house I have built, brick solid,
stucco smooth, stand through the storm,
and stand when I leave, traceless?

Missing *Nyonya* Poster

Where is the *nyonya*
in me gone missing?

Where is the cheeky
chattering girl child born smiling?

Saudara   Emak   Bibik
Scattered last century.
Where is the daughter
                    loving,
beaten   bitter?

Nyonya in the poster
tatters fading
              so long missing
she does not see
herself, *nyonya*,
                    in the figure.

Kuan Yin in California

To bring *Kuan Yin* to California
I did not need ghost money nor joss.
Not altar cloths, sutras, silk embroidered
shoes. The pure eye seizes the image,
near set a heart that asks for images.

Ask and it will be given. To lose,
giving and losing bound like anything,
like man and woman, and nothing,
Zero and Infinite.
                    Where the Goddess
of Mercy born in China, transgendered
from a living Buddha, lifts the jar
of Compassion, I stay thirsty
here in the land of milk and honey.

The Radiance

"Life," Gandhi said, "is a bundle
of duties." Sitting cross-legged
in plain homespun on a clean
mud floor, his face softened
to skull, brown spirit in a small
tender skeleton. So firmly
he spoke, without malice,
without forethought, spirit
of Asia, radiantly toothless,
without book, without self-
epigraph, anonymity
of Asia in cheap glinting glasses.

Beginnings, Queens New York, 1972—

1.   Amber Alert

Shu-fey Wang—seventy years,
escaped from Roosevelt Nursing Home—
speaks no English, thinks she's thirteen,
may be looking for Canton.

2.   Lili Ling

Lili Ling—name like telephone ring—,
Amy's mother, is in her garden
among peonies sacred
to Chinese emperors, in Queens.

Bollywood Dreams

(1991)

I want to be a totally
different woman, never mind
I'll look the same, pimply
scars, open pores, grey hair, flat

chest like a bench for pressing
iron. No iron inside
whether running hot or
running, feet cold. No more

export pig iron poetry.
Let me throw out childhood
horrors, tired of the same
old stories, third world audience.

I want comedy, fantasy,
chases around coconut
plantations, those forever
near kisses that ban realism

and down-in-the-mouth pain.
I'm tired of being
a third-world heroine,
malnourished, beaten, although

all of that was true, although true
no longer, although true now

for many who would rather
watch the plump heroine
wiggle by banana fronds
pursued by her singing
chevalier. They are who
is storming is staring, is

beaten, is burned, is cut up,
is sold. And I'm getting
it. Can the suffering
change the movie?

Revisiting Neighbors

(Westchester, New York, December 27, 1992)

TODAY I turn 48, as good a day to begin something new as any other time. Yesterday my neighbor had skinny candles stuck in a nonfat cheesecake for me. My neighbor, no blood relation, no professional colleague, a neighbor from 1980 to 1990. Ten years is a long time to share a geographical space with someone. Four hundred yards down the lane and across a busy country road to grandma's house, to three acres of woods, lawn and landscaped garden. By 48 I've made some friends. How good they are who can tell? The older I grow the less I understand about friendship because the less I understand about myself because the less I trust my own stories shot full of excuses, weak lies that don't take anyone in, that I repeat only to myself—so I can love myself because I am so hard on myself, I love myself because I am so hard on myself. Because I am so hard on myself, I must learn to love myself. I can't tell in my stories the truth from the lies; and worse I'm beginning not to tell in her stories the lies from the truth. My neighbor's house was always groomed, good Christian woman who spaded for foxgloves and coleus, whose pansies blossomed in half-bowl planters. I saw fancy lavender tones. I saw her life in her clutch of porcelain dolls, pewter candle-sticks, in the old washtub welcoming you to a French door interior, Pfaltzgraff China. She was as good as these things that she read about in the newest *Country Kitchens* magazine. I wished myself an American like her, house on display without irony, without doubt. Till I saw her twitch and cry, her hope in a man startled, gone, and of course that must be so, was always so. Doubt cracks the china, tarnishes the pewter, mildews the peonies. We housewives of the interior who bake love daily crush the grains of our beliefs for the leaving, bake caring into ourselves, crying *eat me eat me—I am sweet, I am nourishing*, and wonder why we are so broken, so wasted, so terrified of our image in the night, *new moon with the old moon in her arms*. Doubt must crack my neighbor open before the seeds will sprout.

Revisiting

(Westchester, New York, December 28, 1992)

THEY are widening the road where the bridge hits the intersection, twelve years after the tipsy housewife ran him over on his brand-new motorcycle his mother had begged him not to buy. Her scream broke in the lane above the pines through the closed nursery window where I was nursing my week-old baby. It shrilled into the summer blue skies of Westchester, over the highways and villages of upstate New York till it rang in the permafrost rousing the Arctic foxes white in their wild-flowering lairs. That handsome boy of twenty-one who'd sprung out of doors that morning fresh as jam and good as anything in her life with a querulous sick husband, no sex, and not much money. Her scream came out of her mouth like the fox startled by a summer thunderclap. It was vixenish, shivering, a silver streak bolting where I rocked nursing my baby, fastening its teeth on my nipples where my son was suckling,

I couldn't sit *shiva* for him. Even mothers are separated by race. Yet for twelve years, I have sat *shiva* on mornings when the sky turns blue and clear like a scream, an Arctic summer thing that grapples the baby at the breast.

Repetition

(January 3, 1993)

Repetition is a revolving door.
She keeps rushing into herself,
Echoes uttered years ago.

How to spring loose from the massive
Structure is history itself,
Shuttering through escape after escape.

Nothing divine about waking up
Gummy-eyed in a different room.
Geography holds, tears down.

Terror keeps the windows locked
Because terror sleeps in these rooms.

What We Deserve

(1993)

We none of us deserve
to run, to stroll, to dance
to walk on tiptoe, to move
as with waves, as on horses
as carried on palanquins
as winged as propellers,
action rolling, calves pumping
the air, giving way.

We none of us deserve
our gaiety, our laughter
careless chatter, singing voices
telephone gossip, kitchen humming
baptismal chanting
tongues wagging, senses
we none of us deserve.

So she torments herself
and us, the slow child and the quick,
the one who sees and the blind one
the mute and the singer
the dancer and the lame
the one who wants and the one who has
what she and none of us deserve.

Woman with the Broad Feet

Woman with the broad feet
Who goes wherever you wish:

Some roads lead to China
Where you will bind yourself
And find your freedom
The tightest of shoes.

Some roads lead to Peru,
The Andean heights
Of chill glories
Where life is impossible.

Some roads lead to Bali.
The wide sand ends
In salt water. That is the way
Of all Paradise beaches.

Some roads lead to Europe,
Small compartments stuffed with silk,
Porcelain, ivory, gold—the loot
Of empires will constipate your senses.

Some roads lead home.
Those are the most dangerous roads.

Borderless Horizon

(December 5, 2015)

Horizon: the obsessive line.
That which haunts.
                    It appears.
Mirage. It disappears.

Unwavering. Constant.
                    Unsteady,
imaginary. Optical illusion.

Imagination: ruler of perspective
where sky and water meet,
sun is born and dies.
                    Where eye
strays, unfaithful to home.

Subversive infinity which
defines, encloses.

The X went up the mountain
to see what she could see.

Seeing the horizon enlarges
the eye. It opens the eye.
Eye encloses it.
Eye and horizon are one
contradiction.

If you cannot approach the horizon,
how can you believe in it? How can
you not believe in its simple straight
distant vision?

Believe in horizons that remain
hanging between here and forever
there. Ever there.

On the Hudson Line, 2008

Three ducks bob in a row, quack past,
six more following yards apart.
June on the Hudson, new families
trail invisible links, not separate.

I wait for the train alone before
commuters merge in mist, combed, shaved,
and coated. We sit in the cars, mere glass
away from brown riverine waves.

Intervals vanished, I am carried
rickety-rock to Grand Central, done
this ferrying not yet too many times,
this morning's journey not yet worn.

The city calls by broad waters,
a companion viewed uneasily,
known as no friend to unbuoyant
bodies, minds dis-intimate. We

fill cars, shut-in faces locked down
on tiny squares bearing daisy-
chain stories for each other, should we speak.
Should we speak, should down-pressed heavy

bodies, ties loosened, shoes unlaced, scarves
(night's sleep like tears) shed, eyes
meeting above trailing ducks in June
bobbing on waves of light rise,

fingers not twitching, mouths not slackened,
not palming furrowed brows, while
links of cars stink underground,
rumble, slowing, grinding for arrival.

Wording America

For Anca Vlasopolos

Sweetgums' spiky pods expel seeds.
I'd sighted them underfoot for years,
only named when a friend proffered
it. Every morning since, underfoot,
I name them to thank the friend who
blessed me with words for seeing.

     So it is with others:
"Oy vez mir!" the Yiddish lament
who married me, inheriting
his grandmother's sighs, *oy, oy!*
a rope I throw into each day's
surging rapids, till he, the *mensch*,
must laugh at the crone he hadn't
intended to wed, marrying
the stranger.

    And *Oh, say can you see*—
words learned for the interview
with the Immigration Man
who wanted proof of my English
and love for *the land of the free,*
my coward's tail sallow-pale
like a quavering voice, knowing
I would be turned out of the *home
of the brave,* my lying tongue
stumbling—dates and forefathers'
names—, freedom's bell in my ears
to sound me into America.

Dear Madam

Dear Madam, we've voted (some of us)
to thank you: figs, loquats, oranges,
mint, etcetera, your care packages
arriving like clockwork. Which does
work for you, turning hours to season,
to spans of anniversaries,
speeding on to light years, where someone
is to meet us, for all we know, waiting.
Whom you are also mothering,
dear Madam, whose mysteries
brush meaning from wind-fallen
fruit and crippled branches.

Unmaking Eve

Perhaps I am not woman
after all. Perhaps another
grounds below woe and man—

a voice singing off-key
in childhood and later
a body dancing to be

alone, howling at the moon,
happy to be unhappy,
who dictates notes, her boon,

poetry that may frame
plots overthrowing the old name.

Dawn

Infant sky glows
>> pink at the day's edges.
Spring's white masses
>> blossom on pear trees bare
a week ago.
>> Cars and heavy-breathing
trucks do not
>> acknowledge changes.
I make up for
>> disrespecting Busy-ness,
its wheels spinning
>> onto ramps and away
from freeways.
>> Someone needs to greet air,
flesh tinted,
>> Santa Ynez ridges'
thirsty bronze,
>> this sacred dawn poem
waking to day.

West Coast

The dark woods straggle in a thin line
we call the green belt, although it holds
nothing up, knots nothing together.

The cracked tarmac trail tracks canopies
like a frayed rope. On the other side,
each morning we mark increase on the street.

Split spaced, a low fence is pulled down,
a high wall plastered in its place.
That bungalow's effaced. Cape Cod

white blue trimmed gables crown the new
owners in love with East Coast living.
Plenty is to be respected. Myriad

ants hove in a lavender spike we picked.
Despite best intentions to respect
gardens, we forget our promises

and pick more violet-blue. Stellar
distances near, as drought, flood, fires, war
and waste take the deep woods over.

Appear

Does the moon appear
                beautiful wherever
it appears, viewed
                through a mind tuned
to light and distance?
                Do we long beyond wherever
it appears, tuned
                to dim and distance?
The close and near
                suffice as breath expands
and world contracts to here
                and its beauty.

Mistress

The inner-most questing
serves silence.
The out-most grasping
for loud acclaim
serves to sell the shackled self.
Choose then the one
that loves you best.

A Short History in Food

Yellow tang in the evening curry pot,
turmeric root wrenched from a *kampong* plot:
the tongue's myth of taste, mother's Malay
murmurs repeated in her child's mouth each day.

Thirteenth free in baker's dozen: *Zabar* aisles'
bagels, midnight steaming, tossed onto piles,
greed and loneliness thick like dust motes,
dense with city singles clenching dollar notes.

On sidewalks oranges and lemons lie, not yet
dismissed in this new garden, too many to pocket.

Remodeled Kitchen

Dear kitchen—perhaps not so dear—,
near thrice ten years my roost and ruse
for life! When some, like Caesar, seek
to conquer all Gaul, you stored garlic
and leeks, appeasing the populace.
You were staged for warring voices,
crashing china, the cabinets oaken-
lined nostalgia parading Indies
spices and blue willow.

                    Restless,
I'd roamed among jars—fenugreek,
garam masala, turmeric, cumin—;
weekly curries all faux, double-oven
Kenmore unused, Chinese stir fries
failing tests of memorization.

Your scrubbed laminate counters,
school of my mid-life education,
ripped, eggshell porcelain cleared,
these little deaths prefigure the clock's
tick-tock, while I fuss, refusing
salad's supremacy for your *Gula Melaka.*

December before Dawn

The year is ending:
early light in late season.
I am pushing it along,
impatient for its ending,
awake before days begin:
cycle in the pea-grit brain
off-cycle, cycle in life
off-kilter, waiting
for the future to kick in.

Song

Oboes, quavering, blow.
The flutes trace memories,
such dreams forgotten soon
as they halt. Querulous
tympani battle. The cello
pleads, *Calm*, that the violins'
pizzicatos do not allow.
Over trumpets' dolorous
or triumphal calls to action,
the tenor caresses the air.
The beloved lives, and does,
so long as his voice pulses
timbres that drift, echo,
as the page closes on the score.

Paying Attention

(For Charles)

The pleasure of paying attention
as if a cloud
of harpists happily appears.

Or the baby
yawns, gums glistening
like abalone shell
picked up after El Nino
storm.

Or your chest rising
and falling, a coastline
secured.

Details
are all I have: grizzled head,
shell, baby,
cloud-borne spirits ungraspable.

Except for yawn, tint, breath
of sleeper on my cheek,
the pleasure of imagining
harpists to whom attention
must be paid.

The cloud closing
with thunder burst,

attention must be paid
to the hostage-taker,
Ephemeral, for whom
details convey down,
dull and dullness,
to final absence.

Particulars parting ways,
atoms splitting,
attention is consoled,
dark and shining
star dust unchanged.

Ripeness

Ripeness—a dry creek is all of spring.
A creek, dry, is all of spring ripeness.
All spring's dry ripeness—a creek.
A creek is all of spring's dry ripeness.
Dry—is all ripeness of a spring creek?
Spring: all ripeness a creek—dry.

Onward!

Where else, how else?
The thousands-footed creature
cannot step backwards. Falls,
struggles, will rise
if the thousands feet
move forward. As
the foot of words
moves, breath by breath,
the roots of words,
grounded everywhere,
arriving here,
the poem writes onward.

EGGSHELLS

Heat Seeker

(9/11, on hearing of the Twin Towers' collapse)

Heat seeker, blood sucker, the smell
of flesh rouses you. Micro
jet fighter buzzing California
airspace between my ears, reconnoiter
of giant jumbled pillows, sheets,
quilts and shams. Unerring, drawn
by ripeness crunched and fearful
under your sting, the long persistent
whine of you, love mosquito,
bearer of news from interiors
I've shied away from. Too late you've
waked me with news of war. Your high
hum startles like the pitch of Harleys
and SUVs, delicate shrapnel
piercing this flesh wrapped in softness
and warmth purchased with a life
exacted for these goods. I've wrapped
myself in white sheets to absolve
me of your sting, my stray muse.
Little black vampire, you eat me
in sips, dodging my ferocity
my gusting sighs. You find the
sweetest side, the honey sliver
between winding sheets, bursting scarlet
to your bite. This is death, a series
of deaths, in our complicated night.

Eggshells

Of eighteen cupped in Styrofoam,
ruled by superstition I place
eight in a pot, watch the cold water
roil, wait for white and yellow
to firm, hard-boil, cool, before tapping
shells against the countertop, peeling
along cracks, letting minutes pass, just
as I'd watched the sky blanch this morning,
fragile, walking as if on eggshells,
roiled in heat we can't withstand, pressed
by an iron, with crackling ground,
Sun a mouth swallowing both
Woman and Earth, yolk and pitted fruit.

The Long Arc

"The arc of the moral universe is long, but it bends toward justice."
—Theodore Parker/Martin Luther King, Jr.

The long arc that was bent
has snapped,
hangs
loose rope swinging.

We're fit to be tied.
Aws
and worse.

Gape.
The rope that sang
divine tension

pleasingly bow-tied,
now noosed
for you.

Plain spoken
poetry has no home.

Ropes strung
in marble lobbies
dismiss the hopeless
hopes broken

for those who'll
never thread
the eye of a needle.

The Hat

Rabbit jumps out of its hat:
a hard pea in a soft breast.
She sweats on her Princess mattress.
Horsemen of the Apocalypse
gallop twenty-four seven
when Rabbit jumps out of its hat.

Rabbit is sprung from its hat:
mushrooms glow on the roof of the world.
Who knows where the kingdom's keys are kept?
The kleptomaniac gives
versions for hares to chase
as Rabbit is sprung from its hat.

Rabbit escapes from its hat.
Claws unclipped for millennia
dig through clay floors and skitter
on marble. Pandora sleeps
now her box is empty,
rabbit escaped from its hat.

Don Giovanni in the U.S.

He grabs pussy wherever he goes,
boasting lists of women seduced
by money, name, and rank. Leporello
has his back, sentinel, watchman, deuce
to the ace. His act is smoothly raw
on the other side of reality's screen.
Miss America Zerlina swoons
to visions of wine and ham, screams
trifling against chocolate truffles
stuffed in her mouth. He caresses
as his aria swells and muffles.
Manor and manner mixed with murder
win our ears. No ghosts, hell-holes, witches
will halt the monkey playing its grinder.

Twenty Sixteen

"It's literally people's lives on the line here."
Elizabeth Warren, June 9, 2016

Twenty sixteen was when the rot showed up.
Neighbors I'd thought nice turned mean, prodded
other folks, like the Doberman Pincher pup

I'd nuzzled, warm and sweet, now muscle-cusped,
fanged—the woman who'd helloed and nodded.
Twenty sixteen was when the rot showed up.

First, it was laughs. The comics turning up,
talk shows mouthing off, the few who lorded
others, like the Doberman Pincher pup

gets all the attention: beefy treats, cups
of ice cream shared, marrow-bones hoarded,
till twenty sixteen when the rot showed up.

Suddenly it wasn't funny. *Hup hup*
of militia, empty houses boarded,
and like the Doberman Pincher pup

trained to meanness, their finger flips no flub
now votes counted, their America guarded,
twenty sixteen was when the rot showed up,
startling in a Doberman Pincher pup.

New Old News

(December 2, 2016)

The card I need to write, address,
and post is under the book I need
to read for the citation I need
for the paper I need to submit;
the book that is under the iPad
I need to update for apps I need
to download, for the travel I need
to plan for the flight to Canada,
is under clippings I need to toss
along with news they cover: old
news of an old America,
wild western civilization
I had swept under the carpet
of mythical history that now
covers card, book, iPad,
clippings of today's new old
news there's no overtopping.

Erosion

(Martin Luther King, Jr. Day, 2017)

The creek is dry another
January. Yesterday, water
channeling, we stopped on the little
bridge to gawk at the scribble
tracing over its bed.
                        Then nothing.
Like a pen drying, the writing
illegible, rhythms too blank
to catch, roots shrivel on their bank.
Slowly, trust obscured, faith bleaks,
erodes, without rain, full running creeks.

Why Is It?

It isn't age that weighs down shoulders.
It isn't lead that wearies feet.
It isn't tongue that speaks falsehoods.
It isn't eyes that look away to spy.
It isn't fog that grays cities.
It isn't sun that burns land to desert.
It isn't fires that crumble trees to ash.
It isn't rains that tumble boulders.
It isn't the pan that blackens meat.
It isn't night that stirs ghosts.
It isn't ghosts that gibberish in light.
It isn't children who've grown unworthy.
It isn't flowers that won't bear fruit.
It isn't Earth that will poison its creatures.
It isn't the creatures that will extinguish.
Why is it?

If

(Inauguration Day, Jan 20, 2021)

If we build reinforced fences higher,
secure miles in rolls of barbed wire,
will we, fetus-curled, sleep any safer?
If we bend lower, even lower,
till, disappearing speck, trenches swallow,
bury us, could we be any safer?
If eyes down, arms raised to surrender
not to mourning but to might to sever
bonds, will we be together any safer?
If we do all this, be all thus,
can we be safer in our cause?
Envoi
If I write another page, another
poem, collect a fancier figure,
can plain thought be lovelier?

Eating Crow

The crow I fed with flesh stripped
from my skin
                    shining blue black crow
whose caw rose from a craw raw
with bully boy joy; wrangling
dismal night strewn, whose strut
and stamp set pulse affright in
pigeons, jays, wrens and starlings

condemns all that glories us,
glories all I condemn.
                    Crow
that scatters morning's bright
white gleaming shell now tears
at my crop as I, gagging,
choke, eating the crow I'd fed.

Value

Mongering has gone out of cycle:
Fishmonger who tossed slippery flounder,
un-gutted, into my mother's basket;
Ironmonger who soldered battered
pans with a fiery rod; my favorite
Newspaper monger who rang his bell
for months' old news, cents to the weight,
carted away on his bicycle.

Today, new mongers seize our news
with old venerable gods: Fear, his troupe—-
Rumor, War, and Hate—borne to view,
traded in households, grouped
saviors for their souvenir picture,
branding with burning cross our future.

School Shooting

the screaming does not stop
                    the silence
                              goes on
    never
            again
                    to touch
    love goes
            on
                    the dying
    the screaming
                    does not stop.

In the long run

poetry will not save,
nor courage, nor love,
less house and hosen,
wealth and its haven.

Prepare for the end,
cries the idiot, raving
on the street corner
as we scamper

with mice and men past
the truth-bearing jaws
of the Great Idiot
patient trapper, Fate.

Night Clamor

Night clamor, silence heavy
as wool under quilt, wakes you,
shakes your mind's frame like a beast
in its cage. Rain has fallen
mute through the hours, steady,
breaking the drought, the hard flue
of baked earth, and now night's yeast
rises in your breath, sour-sullen
with fears—for the future the mother
will not nurture, the wife cannot
care, the teacher will no longer
teach, the eons the body will rot—,
before morning raises the sun,
and I rise, work to be done.

The Lie

The lie I've been telling myself is pen
and paper can take down addresses
fast as rocks, trees & lovers can announce
them. Writing, I'll find my way
back to that rock in Lisbon with lichen.

Ah, but the children keep moving out
of your house, out of town, keep
hiding their real homes, put up signs
"No one's home," and do not read
your postcards. Pen and paper will not
hold them anchored to liquefying
ground.
        The lovers are now fixed
in addresses to which postmen cannot
go, where poems of paper and pen do
no good, even when offered,
burnt, read in propitiatory smoke.

Crick Crack

Crick crack, step
on a crack.
A mind slips.
A pen hacks.
Your breath gasps.
Your hand grasps,
misses. Leaks
ink on page,
leaking blots.
Here comes age.
Words stutter.
Stacks clutter.
Knees shredded,
old fashioned
flashes—thoughts
impassioned—
then stumble.
Late bumble
bee in vines
grape-heavy,
on the track.
Drunken bee
of a rhyme,
triple time,
beat cobbled,
feet hobbled.

Blah, Blah, Blah

What noise emits from a fading star
in a quirky blinking galaxy?
The universal chatter *blah, blah, blah.*

Stock market falling, pix of a porn star.
Move along. Nothing here to see
or hear—just another fading star.

Black holes, chitter chatter of nuclear war.
Threats to be or not to be.
Radio static: *blah, blah, blah.*

Self-firing, self-driving, self-selling car,
exceptional self-reliancy!
Spinning off its axis, the wobbling star

set to implode throws brilliance far
out. We who see a tree
fall in a forest of *blah blah blah*

end not with a whimper but with *blah*
and *blah* and *blah* and *blah, blah, blah.*

Daylight Savings

I've lost an Hour. Has anyone seen it? It seems to have slipped away, a runaway child. I call Amber Alert, and the handler laughs at my urgent request. He says politely, keeping his chuckle down, *Your Hour left of her own accord. Can't make her stay home if she doesn't want to. Besides, the whole country has lost an Hour.* The whole country? I thought it was only hard-ups lost their rights, couldn't pay for a hole-in-one. The last time I listened to cable news a minority had lost hold of their right to rights. A larger party found more rights stashed in the right wing of the house. *You see, ma'am,* the handler says, *your Hour is small potatoes. Count yourself lucky your health is good. Emergency just lost many more hours, you understand me?* His voice gets low, a growly whisper. *If you know what's good for you, you'd stop calling Amber Alert. See what I mean? Missus Constitution has been found and is now in the hospital. Don't call again, OK? We're taking good care of Missus Constitution. Twenty-four-hour police by her bedside, so no one's gonna take her. She's under protective custody. Homeland Security's in on the matter. She'll be going through surgery, see, and when she comes out, no one's gonna recognize her, because she won't be looking like a two-hundred-and-forty-year-old crone. She'd be so botoxed you'd think she was an under-aged minor. And she won't need those robes to hide her weight. They can do amazing things with silicone gel. She's not lost, ma'am, just a small alteration, you know, now she's being fixed up real good. So, yeah, suck up your lost hour, and don't call us again.*

Must History?

Must history always be ashes?
Must we always remember only to destroy?
Must nature always die only to rise on our ashes?
Must children always live through love to bitterness?

Must rains always end in drought, drought in floods?
Must soil burn to desert? Must desert blow away in hot winds?
Must their dirt smother farmers' villages and cities' schools?
Must reeds and weeds choke? Must wheat, rice, corn, land's multi-
grains
lose ears deafened by unceasing noise blasting from engines?

Must I always wish for victory, my motor
driven by this gas desired by billions
and must I always be defeated?

Let me survive in this valley
with other travelers, our stalled camaraderie
to kiss joy and greet happiness.

WALKING ALONE

"They paved paradise
And put up a parking lot."

Big Yellow Taxi

Joni Mitchell

Why I Walk Alone

because I am a social melancholic.
because I am a workaholic.
because walking is a way of working,
and because I work best alone.
because I love to talk
and because sometimes I must talk to myself.
because I dress down when I walk,
dressing down to my naked core.
because walking is a happiness for a solitary.
because pacing with two or three or more
is aggravating to soles.
because the breeze is lighter
without heavy human huffing,
and because steps are lighter
without heavy human sharing.
because I make bad decisions when I walk,
like running when lights turn orange,
because it is okay to kill myself but not you.
because I am more patient when I walk
and because I am impatient when I have to stop walking.
because walking is a dreamer's route
and it is impossible for a companion
to dream the same dream at the same moment
on the same route, wandering away
from madness, separation, despair, home.

Mixed Weather Sestina

The gray gathering hung low in the sky
all day. The expensive pen would not write
unless pressed hard, released, then ran dry
after a sentence. Not a life sentence.
Life was hard labor and the best to be
hoped for: climate change and mixed weather.

First it was cold, wet, pelting weather,
then humid. You'd swear the sunny blue sky
perfect except it would not end. It would be
sixty days high cirrus, clouds that write
of cloudless time. We scribble sentences
before the lakes and rivers, our ink, run dry.

Thursday's Child

Thursday's child is out again
in rain and shine, white in her hair,
home and homelessness still ahead,
unsure which is the dream.

She thinks the answer is
inevitable. No one chooses,
despite the ballot booth,
voices of authority

and power who promise the land
before her. She's walked down the road,
stranded, travel-wrecked, past
shut gates behind which no one

appears. She's never rung the bell
declaring, *Here I am in your
promised land.* Born in a caul
that stung, tongue blistered, she's

moving from elsewhere to elsewhere,
each homecoming a pilgrim's stay.

In Praise of Defeat

Someone needs to take
its part on a planet where
winning's everything.

Leftovers

Keep chilled.
Do not leave on counter.
Consume soon.
Sometimes it is better the day after.
Saving it over time turns it toxic.
It sheens yellow or green or purple
Like a bruise over time.
Leftover love,
Best discarded.

Packing

I am doing this everyday
having learned from Mother,
who packed before she disappeared
to a place I could not imagine:
our lives estranged I did not know
Sorrow when she sat down beside me.

Or from Father who never left.
He grew smaller, crowded with new
babies he welcomed as if with fire-
crackers each year.

                I had to leave
to find a room of my own. What did
I pack, a harried daughter
who carried no suitcase, no backpack,
baggage in my head stored
for life?
           I'm packing again
for a room not my own, families
not my own, stuff no one needs,
luggage in the head still there,
that can't be tagged. Lighter
than air, vacuum-sealed, trash turned
treasure a hoarder cannot live without.

How To Find Your Things

Put everything in its place. A place
for each thing. This box for keys—
automatic garage doors, repurposed

rooms, front house entry in another state.
This drawer for napkins, unmatched, threes,
nines. Cable wires, coiled serpents in baskets

nestle, unpowered. Places proliferate
like tumors, each thing falling out of place.
The more places the more hiding spaces. Yet

you remain a pair of hands, two cranky
knees, one crumbling spine. A box to save
boxes in. Bin for cloth, canvas, plasticky

bags printed with wise sayings, bearing years
(2010, 1986),
sights (Paris, Seoul, Berlin, Syria).

Everything in its place—extinguished
time, urgent papers, name cards—faces mixed,
fleeting, blurry, unrecognized. Vanquished

spaces not for repurposing—pleather
buttoned-up pocket purses, water-proof-lined
for sea crossings (documents unzipped

push open port gates across borders),
tissues for when the crying begins,
bread rolls from the last breakfast cover,

in case lunch and dinner will not appear,
the road you will be walking
holds closed doors of homes—there, here—

that want nothing to do with you, a thing
without its place in a world settling
and selling a place for everything.

Hoarders' Dreams

Hoarding's what we do, like Nature weather.
Bottles, bric-a-brac, unmatched serving ware,
nothing's waste. In our dreams, all things matter,

even what's chipped. Keeping gives us pleasure.
Why toss when we can mend again to wear?
Hoarding's what we do, like Nature weather.

Women before fleeing hide scant treasure
from ruinous men, their bodies left to bear
the nothing that's waste, when few things matter.

Receipts, children's letters, tarnished silver,
worn sneakers: overstuffed closets declare
hoarding's what we do, like Nature weather.

Saving trivia is like turning chatter
to pure drama. Alchemically, where
nothing's waste, dreams (but which?) must matter.

Our mindful hands, detectors that hover
in minefields, pile on piles. Spilling there,
hoarding's what we do, like Nature weather,
where nothing's waste, and stuff in dreams matter.

No Accounting

Pulse, Orlando, June 2016

One's sunny, the other dark. No accounting,
So close together, yet split apart,
Mess being itself our entire meaning.

Fear every moment, hope springs each morning:
The words push out of a single heart,
Some sunny, others dark. There's no accounting.

Rooms are impassable with hoarding,
Fraying, chipped, gorgeous, origins lost. What
Mysteries are hiding in their meaning?

Solitaries serve stories for re-telling
Tales with readers' and writers' parts:
Sunny, dark; dark, sunny. There's no accounting

When and how we begin, why the ending,
Where imagination fails or can only start
Up the mess that is all of meaning.

We reach, hand over hand over heart
Over ocean and horizon to the art
Of the sunny and the dark: no accounting
For mess being our entire meaning.

Goddess of Economy Plus

She's the Goddess of Economy Plus,
can fold legs and arms accordion-wise,
collapse metal trays to disappear,
and blast wintry airs of exhaled dust.

She's scholar of Air Trains' track and cart;
can figure minutes before doors slam shut.
She maximizes to unite the miles,
cadges cyber dollars, hedges to start
and end each flight fed and well rested.

Icarus winged studies, careless, before
he failed and crashed. He lost.
                                    She soars,
roaming the tax-free stores to score.
For fallen Ike she no longer cries,
but frequent flies to shop the friendly skies.

Re-Echoing Westchester

New York, 2010

She sees signs she had missed when she lived there.

    Where?

Roads—*Revolutionary, Washington, David.*

    Id.

Bank signs proclaim "*No Credit Needed*."

    Needed.

Driveways sweep by robber barons' estates.

    Gates.

Lawns spiked with grottos, lakes, ha-ha's, follies.

    Follies.

Where she lives now, SoCal elite wannabes

    (bees),

name streets *Harvard, Yale, Stanford, Berkeley.*

    Whacky!

Plastics litter their beaches. Here, in Arcadia,

    beer!

she parks the rental car at Stop and Shop,

    shop

for a picnic lunch, past two aisles dog food,

    food!

cat food, litter, pet pillows, toys, and treats.

    Treats!

Five aisles frozen pizza, ice cream, Klondike sandwich.

    Which?

Three aisles paper, party goods, Hallmark Cards poetry.

    Poetry?

No gin, rum, or cherry brandy, no wine.

    Whine.

Here and there, U.S. flags flap in the wind.

    Wind

blowing, as Dylan sang, by drive-in ATMs,

    temps,

"*Times they are a-changing*": Doomsday Clock—Tick, Tick,

    Tick.

Denial

on her refrigerator door *is not*
a river in Egypt. She laughs at the magnet
for her broken marriage, plummet
from *zaftig* joy to anorexia.
Once an authentic American story,
gospel faith & bible studies
to save the nation's soul, ideals
of adoring wife, co-counseling couples,
the corporate-profit father model,
till hot April Easter, struggling,
he says, *I need more space*, confessing.
Now her hollow cheeks, new curls combed,
and brownie smiles will not let him home.

Long-Distance Freedom

Long-distance is child
to long-sightedness,
snapping strings tied
too tightly. Tattering
heavy weave to threadbare.
Longsighted holds horizons,
withdrawing the closer
we approach. Horizons
are by nature long distance:
lines in mind ruled for
longing, sunrises ordering
hope, sunsets desiring
soft beds. Long distance has
kept us separate,
uneasily sleeping,
to wake when malice
does not reach, where we
begin, undimmed, free
beyond Envy's horizon.

Power of Names

Everyone has names for those
who are not them.
                    Not human. Not us.
Kwai—dogs and ghosts—we Chinese
call non-people. Some of these
Americans in turn like to say Chinese
are non-white. Like non-being, non-life.

I do not call myself some names: wife,
beauty, saint, poet, and hate the life
in naming. *Chink, Prof, Hey you.* Not I!
"Read me, read me," I want to cry.
My son wraps me in his arms
and says, "I love you, Mom."

Eyeing

Crow grips high wire,
black feathers askew,
cawing as the heat
rises from tarmac
that's cracked all early
summer.
      The loud flocks,
who knows where, have flown.

It perches alone
as I pass, retreat
below, exactly
there, that moment tracked,

crow eyeing with me,
the hot road my wire
here, white hair askew.

Pen to Paper

Pen to paper is not like riding
a bike: the body has not learned it
in joints and sinews, the wheels
do not turn slower, faster. Balance

does not arrive before the nick
of time, as if it had been the knees'
companion forever—trustworthy,
never rusty creaking. Pen to paper

is not easy as getting on a bike,
memory in the spine
steadying what would tip over,
earth-bound, spikes bent. Hand

that holds pen shakes, pauses.
Rheum fills lines and erases
before ink appears, unwritten,
if pen will not practice on paper.

Shadow

Shadow of a bird
on grassy verge
says something about
the weight of a preposition
in how we weigh
a shadow—a thumb
on the morning's scale,
in the price of a moment's
passing, wrapped in
memory's paper.

Shadow of a body
on the mind's verge
says something about
the weight of the preposition
in how we weigh
its shadow—hard-pressed
silence on the heart,
of a life's passing,
masked as paper.

In Silence

1. Winter Moon

This winter moon, bright blot, exits the sky.
I wander, stolen by inconstancy.
Ebb and glut fade into years. Mother Moon,
cradle then word starlight to creation.

2. If It Will Write

No paper at hand, the words pacing,
meter faltering, untraceable
seconds slip un-scanned: the poem, unpaged,
on no page with all that can never return,
that was loving undone. The hand that holds
the pen firms its own firmament,
a past held fast, the placeless placed.

3. On The Page

"It would help to mark the pages," he says,
flipping cover to cover, mouth close to mic.
Bald, portly, he leans into the muse,
kissing his life, his long-lost mother, like
he's a child before us, we laughing, stunned
by his nakedness, to share with strangers
what he'd never given her, resenting
her misery, reserve he didn't want,
she hadn't meant to gift him, existence
of an only child against muteness,
silence of a soul he knows does not exist,
the soul that is, not his dumb muteness.
Excepting here, amplified by wine and crowd.
Here. Before us. Here, on the page, black, proud.

4. On The Page
              one is waiting
words hopeful, brimming to empty.
It's late. You linger, not meaning
to keep one on the page waiting,
while you waver, anxious, shifting
the stresses till blanks declare: Be
on the page! One is waiting,
hopeful, word-full, brimming, emptied.

5. To Writing
Writing, that grew strangeness and love
of strangeness, sang together music
and noise unequal to my fixed
page choreography. She, basic
and first, grows weary, and I
am at a loss as how to physic
her. She has no appetite for Fancy's sweets.
Lists of what's forbidden lengthen
as she slips from the itinerary
I can't put down, estranged, sullen.

6. Writing In Silence
silence not the mind
              chattering in the outer cold,
cold not the loneliness
       of years without a sound,
sound not the soot
       of fires long burned out.
soot not the muteness
              of women who've forgotten speech,
speech not the room you enter,
       blank squares where portraits were hung.
portraits not the poems
       hooded in silence, although
the poem writes in silence.

Faceless

What Facebook cannot record:
the pleasure of being faceless,
an atom in the sunlight
that is an atom in a universe
an atom in the universality
of dust.
                Under the ocean's weight
a crevice un-glimpsable
from Princess cruises held by
the buoyancy of water
that is the faith in all voyaging.
Faith in the crevice within
bodies into which all things
fall: milk and bitter wine dregs,
lees of years held deep in the body
Imagine the holes that pierce,
the crevices under Facebook's
oceanic weight, un-glimpsable
selfies, invisible posts,
possibilities of being an atom,
one atom in a shining text
that is one atom in a universe
that is an atom in the universality
of mysterious dust.

Hunter-Gatherer Now

Hunting, gathering, now on to sorting
the sorts of time past and present.
                                    To come
is to fear. Meantime, sorting what had been
gathered ungathers for others' pleasure:
my treasure islands compacted bazaars,
borne home to rudder and anchor,
till home grounds on silt, fossilizes
to sand. Stratifies.
                        The body, bone
and aerated blood, squats among boxes
sorting its self-editions, memory stones
metamorphosed to trinkets, thrifted years
expended in hunting and gathering,
compressed today in cardboard junk.

.

Marine Layer

Neither rain nor sun,
it hangs, a curtain of wet
through which November
birds, neither nester
nor fledgling, fly
pursuing play. The risen sun's invisible
behind morning's grimacing
pumpkins, like the long-legged
school children illegible
behind masks, waiting,
buses belated by this Pacific
assertion of rising
marine layers, while we,
no longer amphibian,
breathe the salt-flecked air,
grateful for this day's half-glass
filled with human living.

Raptured

Falling, fallen, leaves
 brown-bruised wrinkly:
too many to count
 while the news' obituaries
mark bodies
 lain in cemeteries.
Voices from a chip
 arrive from a century
ago, *tessitura*
 soaring higher than
ear can hear,
 diminuendo threading
silence of deathless
 art. Treading
leaves among scudding
 notes that scan
in sheets lively fingers
 pegged eras
past we are raptured
 to mortality.

Pulse & Flow

It's always either/or, neither/nor, unless it is pulse & flow. I eavesdrop to learn this at the pharmacy, seated on the public blood pressure monitor, deep breathing, eyes shut. Slow the pulse, meditate myself back to security. The line that forms speaks: date of birth, prescribing doctor, covering insurance. *I guess I'll pay for it*, Dorothy Parker quips, leaning on her walker, spine curved. The man, belly jutting, is too flushed for good news. Everyone shuffles in turn, U.S.A. pill nation, and me writing down numbers, tracking how mood shifts track numbers up and up.

I claim ordinariness, pleased to be remarkable in modesty, as every human is ordinary. But no, every human is extraordinary. As I am, each a one. A one, each extra secret and public ordinary agent. Disguise of sameness hides each one's monstrous difference, down to finger whorls, the blood stream helix that spouts from the cut thumb, ordinary crimson extraordinary to the one cut.

The poem is the still point in a turning world. Light is the still point in the turning world. Flesh fails, but light stays. From light to light, mind becomes spirit becomes soul. Pulse flashes and light flows.

Dark is light in a different form. The image appears when the negative operates.

At the pharmacist, identity must be known and given. No ambivalence or ambiguity accepted. At the clinic, sometimes co-payment is needed, sometimes not. Who can keep in mind when and why except the machine?

At the Ridley-Tree Cancer Center, the receptionists have name tags that say "We Care." If I drop my middle name, the world I walk into blooms with life. Name tags declare "We Care" before I am asked for name, date of birth, change in residence. The last may have changed to Nursing Home, Hospice, Serenity House. The more tranquil the naming the closer to terminus. I am given documents to review and sign, waivers, identities not waived, disclaimers, claimants, payment up front, cheques, credit card. I've never seen a patient offer cash.

"The flowers are pens," she tells me, gesturing. Her jar is stiff with plastic petals that sign legible blue and black ink. Everyone smiles as she heads to the noiseless machine behind the counter, credit, insurance, identity cards in hand, information needed for surgery wrist-tags and big-toe-tags should I lie on an unheated slab.

Light, water, earth, air: nature is simple. Leaves multiply, varieties of green, massive fronds, uncountable spines, pea-sized a princess may find and palm-sized to shape into cones and cups. Nature is simple, wants little, makes wildly, imagination infinite. Pulse and flow, the heart that throbs and the blood that flows.

Repetition is necessary. Repetition is life. Day breaks, night sets. The sky breaks dawn like an egg, cooks night like a sunny-side up for her giant husband. He eats every nightfall, and she breaks an egg each morning.

A poem is the still point. A still point is the poem. It is never either-or, neither-nor. The star shows up and makes the dark universe. The dark shows up and makes the star. Each shows and makes the other. That which you are not shows and makes you. You are what shows and makes that which you are not. Spinning in a helix, the still point and the poem, you and who you are not.

As you button, so can you unbutton. What you do, you can undo. Regret is a call to act. Breathing is an act. Holding your breath is hopeless. Release and reset. Shut down and reset.

The hurt child will always be hurt. But she will grow up to become her good mother.

Would I live in their light?

Stars shine, astigmatic distant, happiest
bright views, steady dim, near almost to touch
while comets that trail tails fail, fall. I praise all.

Would I see them if I were hungry?
Would I watch them if I were cold?
Would I welcome them if I were ill?

Would I rise to their nearness if I were shelter-less?
Would I dance with their twinkles if I were crippled?
Would I drink to their nature if I were thirsty?

Would I praise them through years of poverty?
Would I turn to stars on television if I were untaught?
Would I live in their light as I do now, American safe.

Poet's Confession

I am a poet. I get everything
wrong. Love is actually pain may be love.
Today is already yesterday. Tomorrow,
too late, never comes. You are (prove
it!) seldom you, often mistaken for me,
who doesn't know who I am, whose
existence is existentialist
doubtful. Life's meaning is also dubious,
essentially a question that's hardly
questioned.

           Who gets it are not poets,
are whom a poet disdains like she disdains
grammar. Except when she needs it
for crafting meaning, some meaning, a few
meanings: a right and wrong meaning,
except as I get everything wrong.
At least I'm right about this one thing.

Which is more than those who are not poets
can be graded on, who get even that wrong,
who figure they are right, righteous, never
wrong, guided by everything strong:
by self or idea or profit or God, or blessed
by love. Ah, I grant them that happiness.

DAWNS TOMORROW

Scheherazade: "It is nothing compared
to the tale I will tell if I live tomorrow."

Was die Raupe Ende der Welt nennt,
nennt der Rest der Welt Schmette

The Hudson River School of Painters

is American identity, I was told.
Never saw why, until that morning
at the Met. Catskills, the green-bodied
and lively river, twining
on canvas, vaster than actual
dimensions: oiled depth, receding
shadows—West Point, Peekskill—,
I'd driven past, tight-assed, anxious,
by eight-wheelers. I'd been killed
nine times over in near crashes.

There, four-framed order secured,
America glows. A waterfall rushes
held up by color for all time.
The man in the blue coat stands quiet
as I do, gazing at rimmed
mountains, clouds' roving light,
like subdued sheep, nature sublime,
domestication sublime.

In these rooms,
Hudson River billow
moves, settles down to nation's
dark, white, brown, yellow:
water, air above, earth underfoot,
restless as genius, fixed, and flow.

My Brain on Szymborska

My brain, near deserted, barren, locked down,
is cramped with greeting cards, with names
I no longer fix a person to, names
with no faces. They died years ago,
or likely passed on to other
states, countries, lives. I'd forgotten them
as I've been forgotten, mere cards
in my frontal cortex.
                                        Then Szymborska
steps in, her poems scarves vivid, multi-
hued. Joseph's coat of many colors
Father had bestowed, above the brothers
who disdained him for his skinny frame
and over-developed brain, throwing him
into a hole, crying, *Die, brat!*
                                        Rescued,
Pharoah's right-hand man, she wrote
a poem to Lenin.
                                        Still, my brain finds space
for Szymborska's coat, here in a closet
with a gap for her garment. Her scarves float
in the wind, colors turning brighter
to warm my cold brain. *Heat!* Not scarves but
flames. They are burning my brain. No longer
deserted, our brains are trees on fire,
crackling, alive, fires that will never
turn ash. Flickering in tongues, Szymborska's
poetry crackles in city squares rubbished
by Pharoah's missiles.

Pippa

Listening to a pert twenty-year old influencer,
Pippa, on television, I have an epiphany—
a word she does not know, but never mind—
I have been living with a pseudonym all my life.
Billy and *George* are able to reach great heights,
but not girls named after Shirley Temple,
golden ringlets starlet on the silver screen
whom my Chinese father adored, and saw
his infant daughter a glorious imitation
of the world's darling daughter.
                              Google pops up
Shirleys in all manner of places, spaces, surreal
alter egos. *Shirley Lims* flash by, media-stereo-
apparitions, mediocre. Forever uncomfortable
in my skin, unsure of identity, blinded, blinkered
in blind alleys, I am baffled when calls echo
Shirley, Shirley, and girls wave sprightly hands, *Me!*
Me! Me!
            Temple rose from Hollywood to diplomacy,
inimitable. I've searched for my real
name; pass up *Polly,* another parrot's shrill
simulacra of voice.
                      Now, somehow, *Pippa*
has struck a chord in my core's haunted house
in which *Pippa* is my road not taken. The path
I took was *Shirley's* road not taken. *Pippa's,*
I feel, staring at the TV screen, should have been
mine, Pippa who fearlessly loses her way
in Angkor Wat or climbing up a city on a hill.

Yet, why two roads, the template imagined
by a man who invented himself to be

who he was not, Farmer Frost in Vermont.
Why not three, hundreds, thousands on thousands
lanes, streets, avenues, trodden trails, wildernesses,
seaways, and riverine tracks?
                              Crossroads keep cropping up
if life is long. Roads not taken at twenty
may be derring-do acts of ignorance. Bravado.
Middle aged, you might decide otherwise—
shady sidewalks ringed with rails rounding
suburban yards more alluring than
adventure trips to harems in Morocco.
What would become of divorce if permitted
one opportunity at risky social arrangements?

One epiphany is too few, except in short stories;
can be overtaken by a second, the second
by a third. Does being overtaken erase the flash
of intuition, suddenly brightening and clearing
an overgrown path? Is the first lover done in by
a second, a first kiss foresworn by a second? No.
We grow into names given, baptized or bowdlerized,
the way sap running through stems grows into
saplings, trees. Spirits roam in haunted houses
looking for names not chipped on stone, for
epiphanies, alternately bearing flowers,
not ashen ghosts but flesh, throbbing with joy.

Dawns Tomorrow

Dawns tomorrow surprise with repetition,
surprise with newness, wrinkles, losses
anticipated, like king tides erasing
the steps of women alert to salt water
rising.
       The sea moves the same tomorrow,
although I have learned, understood,
apprehended future's different
grains and molecules from that scooped
in my tight-clasped palm-bowl.
Today's a sieve no palm can seize.

I stoop to scoop, to psalm those tears
desired. Commonest of salts,
connoisseurs of rare souls hold
them cheap. Exorbitant salt!
I labor to mine the mineral,
no matter footprints buried seconds later.

Prepositions

Am I the only English teacher who
cannot decide which preposition
to use? *To* or *For*? *To give* or *For me*?
Which speaks precisely, and to whom
does it matter?
                    I am a second-tongue
poet, teaching English *as if* it is
native *to* me. Or native *for* me?
A language that gives *to* me and *for* me.

Does anyone else have a problem with
with? Seated *with* him is not quite *by* him.
He helps me *to* a seat; I am seated *by* him.
I sit *with* him; I have seated
myself *by* him. One is passive.
Is my other active voice? Transgressive
voice.
                    I learned *from* Puerto Ricans,
Spanish is not perfect native *in*
the South Bronx. ESL native is imperfect
pre-position, *to-ing* and *fro-ing*.
Native speakers too dislike prepositions.
Press pause as they write, preposterous
to figure *out* such flim-flam grammar.
                    In writing, we are imposters,
guessing at meanings hot off the press,
surmising hypotheses raised to heights
of interpretation, *before* degrading
into error. No language is owned
at birthright, towering Babel, muezzins
calling one hundred and fifty prepositions,
crying *about* Being, fumbling
and tumbling, *within* and *without*.

Deadlines

THERE is a reason why a flat line, static beep of a heart monitor, signals death. No iambic beating heart rhythm, changeful metrical skip, no music of living.

My life was ruled by deadlines. Without them I would not be here, halfway up the ladder. Fear of death by deadlines cramped my lifeline. My son wouldn't obey the obstetrician's deadline. He stayed two weeks longer in Mom's B&B. A scalpel sliced me open to wrench him wailing against the bright world. He was my lifeline who kept pulling me away from deadlines.

Some lines are thin. The thin blue line. Some lines are thin that should be thick. The thin green line. The green belt is pared away by paved tracks, bike paths, dead grass, stone-strewn gopher holes.

Some remain thick that should be thinned. Race. Class. Lines between rich and poor, pale and dark, bodies with different parts, set in different places, rubble and marble.

Think peace waxing thick and thin as if with the moon when it should be a solid eternal, the sun itself.

Who created lines, whether thin, thick, or wavering? The Divine is mobile, from Zeus to swan, from Godhead to bleeding human.

Remembering Water

Dogs I never had is the same reason
for mothers I never had. The first pup,
sweet-speckled brown-white, whimpering
held warm against my chest, sweaty hurrying
home after Convent classes. For weeks droopy
ears wiggled at my secrets, forgiving
unwashed face, bony arms, mended
let-down-hemmed uniform.

                     One
afternoon her warm puppy nose was gone,
disappeared, the way Mother disappeared
without warning, the way I learned years later
humans disappeared in Argentina,
dropped into the Atlantic from which
bodies could never beach, washed ashore.
The way I learned that evening the pup
was dropped into the Malacca River
from where my calls *come to me*
echoed in the noisy Central Market
twilight.
      A mother who never returns,
a dog who disappears, a Second Mother
who disappeared both, the reason
why I've never desired dogs or mothers,
a ten-year-old remembering water.

Hitting the Ground Running

How? Impossible when ground is uneven,
rises steeply, falls away chasm
fissured, or merely cracked, threatens
trip or crash at every other step.
Yet run I must. The woman who leans
on her driving wheel says, "*We are watching
you.*" In other words, *Watch out.* Her screen
is car-wash clean, here on a street I've walked
for over thirty years, blissed by blue
skies of Goleta, fruitful Good Land
sidewalks, lime and avocado strewn,
her harsh voice breaking into an illusion
of neighborhood, today only an Asian
walking alone, my threat to sameness
threatened, my praise song to difference
intercepted by an English sentence.

What Happens?

What happens when it dawns on you
no one you know wants your full disclosure?
What happens when you choose to keep breathing?

What happens when you take your eyes off
the finishing line you've been racing toward?
What happens when you walk instead of running?

What happens when you sit on the sand
and it is dry, and what happens when you
sit on the sand and it is wet?

What happens when you stop listening,
when your hearing gets so bad
and you are happy about it?

What happens when you buy
a sensitive hearing aid, when your neighbors
believe you are hard of hearing?

What happens when your hearing aid
eavesdrops on their pity? What happens
when hearing their pity is hard on you?

What happens when you are living through
the worst drought in one thousand two hundred years,
and neighbors water lawns every other day?

What happens when Santa Barbara
is green-full luscious grass? What happens
when you plant red stones and grow brown mulch?
What happens when you tire of questions,
and question what they mean now and in the past?
What happens when the rain-free blue

morning must mean enough for each day?
What happens when even that enough
asks what happens when enough happens?

Perhaps

	is anachronistic
perhaps	am left with the child whom
perhaps	I grew up to be
perhaps	was peevish, indecisive, dying of curiosity, and quite dissatisfied
perhaps	one day something would happen and then…
perhaps	waved hands in distress but didn't say a word
perhaps	was no princess, so no one cared, and she didn't care either
perhaps	ran a mile, walked down many byways, was lost again and again, perhaps even again
perhaps	walked on the Great Wall in a dream or left with a stranger who'd left her in the first place.

Sunglasses

My super-large expensive Italian
sunglasses' lightweight plastic has
crease-scratches in its lower right lenses.
It covers the ophthalmologist's
prescribed triple-powered glasses —
myopia, driving, distance sighting, —
three diagnoses of vision shredded by
reading, UV ray holes in retinas,
irises burning in smoky cafes,
and wildfire particulate ash.
Protecting what's left of vision,
I double lenses over baggy eyes.
These faint cracklings are like a sky
scratched by the sun, and I a Mad
Hatter walking in the giant oven
outdoors.
        Cracked eggs gone bad,
careless handling is no excuse
for the sad waste of it all. Sunglasses
sit atop my head like my dark self sits
atop me, like weather vanes sit unmoving
atop houses in breathless noon.
No one needs sunglasses costing
more than families' annual groceries
where sun has cracked their rivers.

Does hope stir the weather vane? Will
heat breathe when evenings fall?
Will cradled babies sleep tonight
if the dark self seeks light, light, light?

On living near an airport

Bedroom, hot late July rising summer,
heats with roars of a plane taking off or
landing. Either is an indifferent matter
to the sleeper who cannot sleep, just another
misery, like the midges' tiny crusted bites
that will not heal—little welts at armpits
and shins that expensive ointments have not
soothed despite small print promises. Another
insanity that money does not
understand: the convenience of airports,
the convenience of living near to one.
This itty itchy irritation,
these window rattles, these miseries, annul
the conveniences of living for
the sleeper, deep-dive dreaming cancelled;
so, resigned to the pleasure of awaking,
sipping tea past midnight, to live
without sleep, if necessary to live.

Oak Fire, Mariposa County, 2022

The squirrel leaps and leaps, each more than a foot apart, bounding across black asphalt clear of commuters, over the creek's retaining wall onto a coastal oak branch. The crack I hear cricks of dry-crunchy leaves bearing acorns smaller, less shiny than last year's. Like this squirrel, slenderer than last year's puff-cheeked, fat-tailed, cocked-high, inquisitive, scrambling up brawny trunks.

California was brawny in recent memory. Our memories bear fewer rings than giant sequoias. Red and orange bark, their firemen's uniforms, in the wild flames crash up north where Drought's daughters are set loose to kill what we love. Our American Furies, revenging new-nursed and ancient stalwarts, ring on ring counting years when we autopsy their corpses.

Compassion fatigue

Fingers twitch as the screen hosts infants,
heads enlarged above skeletal limbs,
to press the remote button or sign
another cheque.
We are animated
by yellowing lawns. Poetry
devotees specify life-sustaining
verse and will not read apocalyptic
diction. What then to imagine
if not reality?

The doctor advises
eight hours of sleep. Sleep half wakeful,
tossed on storms of Suffering's
stories, to breakfast on fatigue.

Compassion was once a buffer,
a moat crossing between ladies
and the lame. Drought has dried its water.
Boulders Sisyphus rolled uphill
have tumbled, an effort to clamber
for indefatigable ladies grown
weary of mercy, care fatigued.

Mermaid feet

Her uncropped hair, grey-streaked, uneven,
lanky. Bobbed, free, she's confident here,
buoyed where water is salt. Seamaid, salt flavors
life, and fresh water is rarer than wine.

Nereide, half woman, half fish, thrown by waves,
crawling toward land, grows ankles and toes.
She's flip-flopped over half of Earth, blows
half-Wind Goddess, half kitchen-slave

who spins vane to the weather. Soon,
her calloused feet will crumble,
return to surf, as sand to sand tumbles,
nothing saved of their fifty-two bones.

Perseverance

humans engineered for our agenda,
the Atlas rocket flying past the old
romantic moon to land Rover on
a planet so red ancients saw
Mars' face in its burning soil.
Lifeless, red: Rover, persevering
far from blue-green shimmering
Earth, scrapes rock samples for water
& life signs.
                    Perseverance, a gift
to be earned: more than persistence,
conscientious Type A doubled down,
the gift toiled for—toiling human
knowledge whose gifts come free.
Perseverance, scraping the frozen
cover for proof life once prevailed.

The Fittest

Size doesn't signify, I say brazenly,
smugly. Think of the megalodon,
whose 3-D computer model suggests
a max sixty-five feet length, eons extinct,
set against my five-foot frame. Its speed
three miles an hour a paltry slow boat
compared to my two-door Honda revving
seventy miles, veering past lumbering
sanitary dump trucks. An electric
wheelchair can outrace the beastie.

Survival of the fittest means me,
I crow, despite *tsk-tsking* on our species'
inhumanity, inability
to adjust expectation to reality.
Paleontologists map species types:
apex predators like megalodons
most prey to snake and ladder fall. Evolution
is crammed with irony. The first shall be
last.

       I have never triumphed in a race
or game, sidelined in teams. Quick and nimble
know I drop relay sticks, forget to watch out
for the girl panting up the track.

               Smugness
is in the mirror neurons of homo sapiens,
brawny and brainy, imaging with the Nobel
Prize writers, Fields Mathematics medalists,
the Tour de France cyclists: identity
every apex predator's winning game.

Life is Not an Exam

Life is not an exam. Its multiple
choices don't fail you if you mark an X
in an incorrect box. Your X's do
not box you in. Erase them. Blot them out
with black, red, or green or purple magic
marker. One choice does not prohibit two
other choices. Love all three and they will
love you back, the way a friend loves you
and introduces you to another
you will also love, for no circle
should be complete, the way examination
doors bang shut when you sit down to write
the finality of your learning. Life
is not answers to strangers' questions.
You do not have to recall precisely.
Rosy glasses are acceptable.
Some traumas that fog vision may be wiped
away. There will be no penalty
for misremembering. Some ex-es
are best forgotten, not skulking in cells.
Life is replete with mistakes, and also
with lucky guesses, the way you are wife,
despite failing your driving test, in
someone's lucky life.

No

on refusing the Muse, and not
regretting it, the way I did not
regret not marrying the man
I wanted to marry. Retiring
her abject, domineering,
seductive voice, her promised
desserts at the end of plain
tables of famine. My life-coach nods
just say no, to She who must
be obeyed, who dances naked
bathed in language, renewing
sparks recreating me. *No.*

Murmuration

A charm of hummingbirds

A crackle of grackles

A murder of crows

A clowder of cats and their kindles

A bleep of mf's

A basso nova of bikinis

A sunbeam of babies

A bluster of pundits

An empire of ethnicities

A trauma of traffic jams

A cacophony of department meetings

A depression of divorces

A shaken cocktail of bartenders

An autocracy of a#%holes

A unicorn herd of startups

A hopeful of NGOs

A transgression of teenagers

A Costco of cookies

A wanton Houses of the Rising Sun

A bankruptcy of ideas

or a Pleiades of ideas

A suite of bankers

A beggary of lobbyists

A school of poets, like a school of fish,

is not a shiver, a grind of sharks,

but a collective, foolish & flashy.

Ode to a Sick Bed

Immersed in misery, the mirror,
reflecting a nose doubly swollen
with snot and sneezes, banished from
a room incapacitated for
vanity, O Bed, an anchor
for the day, securing the body
swaddled in sheets, flannel
a torture for bare burning skin,
I have entrusted myself to you,
scattering wet and crumpled tissue,
head blown like a trombone beating
with a metronome of migraine.
To you I can cry, as to a god,
knowing I offend none, your mattress
softly firm as a mother should be,
coverlet storm-tossed as my hair, fever-
damp, Bed rumpled as a chest
lumpy with phlegm. I swallow
palmfuls of pills, sip a little water,
to fall on you, Bed I have not made.

Car Therapist

Driving to the oncologist, I am talking
to myself, a volunteer car therapist.
A speedster cuts to my right
in near collision, forcing a fast brake
which I do, cussing, middle finger waving,
damming him and everything his.

I say loudly, *Calm down, Shirley*. Why,
his wife may be dying, caesarean gone badly,
the obstetrician calls—*hurry, hurry, hurry!*
Or he's a high school graduate, out just June,
lucky to land a job downtown, and he's late,
the boss even now checking the clock.

                    Everyone needs a break,
my car therapist says, *and you are going to
give him one this morning.* Calming nod, agreeing,
fingers crossing: the ultrasound gives me a break.
My trusted oncologist can do only so much
when the body goes crazy and grows new
cells even as it's ageing. Growth at any age
has its pros and cons. Some cons are fatal.
My car therapist talks me kindly through merging
lanes and caffeinated big-rig trucks,
navigating me to my destination.

Arachne

Grandmother spider, eight segmented
legs to scuttle, spin, pin down
another's wings, wrap a cocoon
coffin, what can I learn
from you? Your egg sac drops more
babies in one dry day than
I had bled eggs in more than
twenty years, effortlessly
birthing, effortlessly
mothering. Do I learn to turn
away envy, two eyes, four
limbs, sliced open for one
child? Do I learn devotion
from sisters to earn womankind?
Arachne's eight eyes skein
silks from bare January, tree
to tree, immortality's
multitudinous spiderlings
fine veiling the orangery,
ours to mimic, word to word.

Moment

We all deserve a happy ending,
poor and rich, high-born and runty.
Paradise gleams with early morning
birds pecking at grass seeds in a dry
patch, happy seed in the happy
beak, a moment of morning
happiness, seizing endings as ending.

Acknowledgements

Acknowledgement is made to the following, in which the poems were originally published, some in slightly different form, or are forthcoming:

"How To Find Your Things", "The Hat", "New Old News", "Daylight Saving", "The Hoarder's Dream," *Anglistica*, Special Issue: "Making Sense of Mess: Marginal Lives, Impossible Spaces." Vol. 22, No, 1 (2016).

"Thursday's Child," "Packing," *Hong Kong, 20/20*, Blacksmith Books, 2017.

"Winter Moon," *Journal of Transnational American Studies*, 10.2 (Winter/Spring 2019–2020): p. 163.

"Before and After Leaving Malacca," "Convent Lessons," "Value," "Faceless." "Poet's Confession," "To Writing," "Writing in Silence," "Moment," in "The Value of Arts and Humanities in the Time of the Pandemic," Perspectives (Inaugural issue, November 2020), *International Journal of Asia Pacific Studies*. Retrieved from https://ijaps.usm.my/?page_id=5649

"Don Giovanni" in *Men Matters Online Journal*, Inaugural Issue, December 2020, p.1-2 https://menmattersonlinejournal.com/wp-content/uploads/2020/12/Shirley-Lim.pdf

"Power of Names" & "Missing Nyonya Poster," *Journal of Postcolonial Writing*, Special issue: Malaysia Literature in English, Issue 5, Volume 57, 2021: pp. 723-724, published online: 12 Nov 2021.

"The Hudson School of Painters," *Hudson Review*, 75 th Anniversary Issue, Vol. LXXXVl. Spring 2013, p. 138.

"My Brain of Szymborska," "Prepositions," *Feminist Studies*, Volume 48, Number 3 (2023), pp. 887-889.

"Beginnings (Queens, New York, 1972), Amber Alert, Lili-Ling, Catalogue, The Radiance: Gandhi" "Pippa,"/published as "Epiphanies," "Deadline" *voice & verse*, Issue 69, February 2023, pp. 84-85.

"On Living Near an Airport," "Hitting the Ground Running," *voice & verse*, Issue 70, April 2023, p. 89.

"On the Ferry to Macau," "Convent Lessons," National University of Singapore Morning Run," *Postcolonial Text*, 2023.

"Admiralty," in *Where Else: An International Hong Kong Poetry Anthology*, Ed. Jennifer Wong, Jason Eng Hun Lee and Tim Tim Cheng, Verve, Birmingham, UK (2023): p. 111.

"Plenty," in "Hunger Memories, the Pandemic, and Ethical Eating for the Anthropocene," *good eats: 32 writers on eating ethically.*, ed. Jennifer Cognard-Black and Melissa Goldthwaite, New York University Press: New York, 2024, p. 318.

"Re-echoing Westchester, New York, 2010", "Mixed Weather Sestina", "Oak Fire, Mariposa Country, 2022", "Marine Layer" in *Chant de la Sirene: Journal of Poetry & the Hybrid Arts*. Special Issue, Climate and Nature, Fall, 2023.

"Wording America," "Heat Seeker," *Valley Voices*, V23, Fall 2023, pp. 22-23.

I thank my editor and editorial partner Chryss Yost and George Yatchisin; Lauri Scheyer for her introduction; Dennis Haskell, Julie Kane, Tammy Lai-Ming Ho for their blurbs, friends and colleagues whose support lift me through the decades: my N.Y. Westchester AAUW poetry collective—Karen Erla, Joan Falk, Lilian Joffe, Irene Kleinsinger, Mary Ellen LeClair, Doris Lowenfels, Patricia Roth, and Mary Schenck—, Can Askoy, Vincenzo Bavaro, Boey Kim Cheng, Noelle Brada-Williams, Joan Chang, Kai Hang Cheang, Grace Chin, Daryl Dickson-Carr, Pin-Chia Feng, Shelley Fisher Fishkin, Dana Gioia, Dean Gui, Laura Hinton, Hsinya Huang, Carl Jenks, Klaudia Lee, Leong Liew Geok, Eva Leung, Brandon Liew, Eric Lars Martinsen, Chingyen Mayer, Nina and Peter Morgan, Pauline Newton, Kathy Patterson, John Peavoy, Jon Pedee, Angelia Poon, Stephen Sohn, Tiag Yi Tan, Tan Xiang Yeow, Eddie Tay, Tee Kim Tong, Malachi Edwin Vethamani, Anca Vlasopolos, Jennifer Wong, Chin Ying Wu, John Zheng; my extended Lim family in Malaysia, Singapore, Australia. UK, Canada, and USA; and my family Charles Bazerman and Gershom Kean Bazerman.

ABOUT THE AUTHOR

Shirley Geok-lin Lim received the British Commonwealth Poetry Prize for *Crossing the Peninsula*, making her the first woman and first Asian to receive the prize. She has published eleven poetry collections, most recently *In Praise of Limes, The Irreversible Sun*, and *Ars Poetica for the Day*. She has also published three chapbooks. Her poetry has been widely anthologized and published in journals like *The Hudson Review, Feminist Studies* and *Virginia Quarterly Review*. Her poems have been featured on television by Bill Moyers, on podcasts such as Tracey K. Smith's *Slowdown*, and set to music as libretto for various scores. She received American Book Awards for her edited anthology, *The Forbidden Stitch*, and her memoir, *Among the White Moon Faces*. She has been honored with MELUS and Feminist Press Lifetime Achievement Awards and UCSB's Research Lecturer Award. She is also author of three novels, *The Shirley Lim Collection*, three short story collections, and two critical studies, as well as editing or co-editing well over a dozen anthologies and special issues of journals.

Printed in the USA
CPSIA information can be obtained
at www.ICGtesting.com
LVHW092340140224
771868LV00002B/195